Leadership Strategies
Taught by the Carpenter

By: Susan D. Smith

Leadership Strategies Taught by the Carpenter
By Susan D. Smith

ISBN-13:978-1523746880
ISBN 10:-1523746882

Copyright 2016 Susan D. Smith

Cover Design by Susan D. Smith
Printed in the United States of America.

This book may be purchased online at:
http://amazon.com
and other fine book sellers.

Bookstores and churches, etc., may purchase this book at wholesale for resale or distribution.

Habakkuk 2:2 (KJV)
And the Lord answered me, and said, Write the vision and make it plain upon the tables, that he may run that readeth it.

(This book is not the complete leadership strategies as taught by the carpenter but is complete as developed for the seminars.)

Table of Contents

Strategic Vision

A vision is always the starting point for any great leader. Jesus had a vision, do you?

What does the word vision mean?

As defined by Dictionary.com it states the act or power of anticipating that which will or may come to be

What does the word strategic mean?

It is a plan, method, or series of maneuvers for obtaining a specific goal or result.

What vision did Jesus lay out for the disciples?

What vision did Jesus have for the church?

John 17:13-26 (KJV)
13 And now come I to thee; and these things I speak in the world, that they might have my joy fulfilled in themselves.
14 I have given them thy word; and the world hath hated them, because they are not of the world, even as I am not of the world.
15 I pray not that thou shouldest take them out of the world, but that thou shouldest keep them from the evil.
16 They are not of the world, even as I am not of the world.

17 Sanctify them through thy truth: thy word is truth.

18 As thou hast sent me into the world, even so have I also sent them into the world.

19 And for their sakes I sanctify myself, that they also might be sanctified through the truth.

20 Neither pray I for these alone, but for them also which shall believe on me through their word;

21 That they all may be one; as thou, Father, art in me, and I in thee, that they also may be one in us: that the world may believe that thou hast sent me.

22 And the glory which thou gavest me I have given them; that they may be one, even as we are one:

23 I in them, and thou in me, that they may be made perfect in one; and that the world may know that thou hast sent me, and hast loved them, as thou hast loved me.

24 Father, I will that they also, whom thou hast given me, be with me where I am; that they may behold my glory, which thou hast given me: for thou lovedst me before the foundation of the world.

25 O righteous Father, the world hath not known thee: but I have known thee, and these have known that thou hast sent me.

26 And I have declared unto them thy name, and will declare it: that the love wherewith thou hast loved me may be in them, and I in them.

Let's look at this passage and pull it apart with other passages throughout the Bible to determine what Jesus is saying, what it means and how it affects us today in leadership.

(1) Jesus came for us to have joy fulfilled in ourselves.
(2) Jesus gave us his Word.
(3) He tells us the world will hate us because we are not of the world just as He is not of the world.
(4) Jesus tells us that he is not praying for us to be taken out of the world but for us to be kept from evil.
(5) Jesus again wants us to get the point that we are not of the world just as He is not of the world.
(6) Then he explains we need to be sanctified. We are sanctified by the Word of God.
(7) Jesus says He was sent here just as He is sending us into the world.
(8) Lastly, in this passage He says I sanctify myself so that we might be sanctified through the Word of God.

How do we accomplish the vision Jesus has for the church?

We have to study the Word of God. It has to become as natural to us as breathing. Memorization of the scripture will help us. No matter what you do in leadership these principles Jesus gives us in this passage let us know the basics.

SUMMARIZATION:

Jesus has done the following for us. As ambassadors of Jesus Christ we need to give the following to the people who are helping us accomplish the goals God has given us for our organizations and churches. An Ambassador understands the importance of order and submission. It is a must that we know how to do these things:

BE SUBMITTED

While in this passage obedience or submission is not called out but it is implied over and over again by Jesus in other passages and below in Hebrews it puts it very clearly. This will be covered in more depth under Strategic Actions.

Hebrews 13:17 (KJV)
Obey them that have the rule over you, and submit yourselves: for they watch for your souls, as they that must give account, that they may do it with joy, and not with grief: for that is unprofitable for you.

In leadership we are responsible for those that are following us. All leaders need to be submitted to a leader. You cannot expect the people who follow you to be submitted, if you, are not, at first submitted to authority. In a church leadership role you should be submitted to a pastor. Of course, you should be submitted to God.

BE HAPPY!

Understand God is a strategic thinker. It is important for God's people to understand His Word. It is also important for those that don't believe in God to understand the principles of strategy in the Bible. It will help you to be a better leader.

When working with people it is important to note that people who work with their bosses are happier than those who work for their bosses. Another important point to note is that those who work with bosses who smile are happier. Thereby a much better workplace ensues.

GIVE THE EMPLOYEES THE NECESSARY TOOLS TO PERFORM THE TASK ASSIGNED.

Jesus said He gave us the Word. That is our tool. The Bible is all you need when coupled with prayer. Don't ask anyone to complete tasks without equipping them with the tools they need. It doesn't matter what you ask someone to do as a leader you must make sure you know they have the proper tools to complete the tasks assigned.

DEFINE CLEAR GOALS

In this passage of scripture Jesus gives clear direction. You are being sent into the world. Be sanctified through the Word of God.

How?

To be sanctified through the Word of God you must spend time in the Word of God. When you do it will do the following:

Ephesians 5:26
That he might sanctify and cleanse it with the washing of water by the word,
----

Does our vision line up with the vision Jesus had for the church?

Do we understand the vision Jesus had for the church?

KNOW WHAT YOU ARE FIGHTING AGAINST AND UNDERSTAND IT

Ephesians 6:12-13(KJV)
For we wrestle not against flesh and blood, but against principalities, against powers, against the rulers of the darkness of this world, against spiritual wickedness in high places. Wherefore take unto you the whole armour of God, that ye may be able to withstand in the evil day, and having done all, to stand.

Galatians 5:7 (KJV)
Ye did run well; who did hinder you that ye should not obey the truth?

Strategic Actions

Obedience

1. Value of Obedience

   Matthew 3:13-15
   13. Then cometh Jesus from Galilee to Jordan unto John to be baptized, of him.
   14. But John forbad him, saying, I have need to be baptized of thee, and comest thou to me?
   15. And Jesus answering said unto him, Suffer it to be so now: for thus it becometh us to fulfil all righteousness.

2. Immediate Obedience
   It is good to obey but better to obey immediately.

   Matthew 4:18-22
   18. And Jesus, walking by the sea of Galilee, saw two brethren Simon called Peter, and Andrew his brother, casting a net into the sea: for they were fishers.
   19. And he saith unto them, Follow me, and I will make you fishers of men.
   20. And they straightway left their nets, and followed him.
   21. And going on from thence, he saw other two brethren, James, the son of Zebedee, and John his brother, in a ship with Zebedee their father, mending their nets; and he called them.
   22. And they immediately left the ship and ther father, and followed him.

Thinking out of the Box

Thinking out of the Box propels you to another level of leadership. This level will never be attained as long as you keep doing the same thing day after day. You've got to embrace the impossible making it possible.

Below I am giving two examples of Jesus thinking out of the box.

1. Jesus, a child, teaching in the synagogue. Now, that's thinking outside of the box.

Luke 2:40-52

40. And the child grew, and waxed strong in spirit, filled with wisdom: and the grace of God was upon him.

41. Now his parents went to Jerusalem every year at the feast of the Passover.

42. And when he was twelve years old, they went up to Jerusalem after the custom of the feast.

43. And when they had fulfilled the days, as they returned, the child Jesus tarried behind in Jerusalem; and Joseph and his mother knew not of it.

44. But they, supposing him to have been in the company, went a day's journey; and they sought him among their kinsfolk and acquaintance.

45. And when they found him not, they turned back again to Jerusalem, seeking him.

46. And it came to pass, that after three days they found him in the temple, sitting in the midst of the doctors, both hearing them and asking them questions.

47. And all that heard him were astonished at his understanding and answers.

48. And when they saw him, they were amazed: and his mother said unto him, Son, why hast thou thus dealt with us? behold thy father and I have sought thee sorrowing.

49. And he said unto them, How is it that ye sought me? wist ye not that I must be about my Father's business?

50. And they understood not the saying which he spake unto them.

51. And he went down with them, and came to Nazareth, and was subject unto them: but his mother kept all these sayings in her heart.

52. And Jesus increased in wisdom and stature, and in favour with God and man.

2. Jesus calling the one who was persecuting Christians to be persecuted for his names sake.

Acts 9:1-16

1. And Saul, yet breathing out threatenings and slaughter against the disciples of the Lord went unto the high priest.
2. And desired of him letters to Damascus for the synagogues, that if fe found any of this way, whether they were men or women, he might bring them bound unto Jerusalem.
3. And as he journeyed he came near Damascus: and suddenly there shined round about him a light from heaven:
4. And he fell to the earth, and heard a voice saying unto him, Sal Saul, why persecutest thou me?
5. And he said, Who art thou Lord? And the Lord said, I am Jesus whom thou persecutes: it is hard for thee to kick against the pricks.
6. And he trembling and astonished said Lord, what wilt thou have me to do? And the Lord said unto him, Arise, and go into the city and it shall be told thee what thou must do.
7. And the men which journeyed with him stood speechless, hearing a voice, but seeing no man.
8. And Saul arose from the earth; and when his eyes were opened he saw no man: but they led him by the hand, and brought him into Damascus.
9. And he was three days without sight, and neither did eat nor drink.
10. And there was a certain disciple at Damascus, named Ananias; and to him the Lord in a vision, Ananias. And he said Behold, I am here, Lord.
11. And the Lord said unto him, Arise, and go into the street which is called Straight, and enquire in the house of Judas for one called Saul of Tarsus; for, behold he prayeth.
12. And hath seen in a vision a man named Ananias coming in, and putting his hands on him, that he might receive his sight.
13. Then Ananias answered, Lord, I have heard by many of this man, how much evil he hath done to the saints at Jerusalem:
14. And here, he hath authority from the chief priests to bind all that call on thy name.
15. But the Lord said unto him, Go thy way: for he is a chosen vessel unto me, to bear my name beore the Gentiles, and kings, and the children of Israel:
16. For I will shew him how great things he must suffer for my name's sake.

Self-Control

This is a quality that all leaders must exhibit. As long as we lead people they will cause us to lose our self-control unless we understand the reason for the self-control. We also have to have placed it on an altar. It is important to be angry and sin not.

Matthew 5:21-26
21. Ye have heard that it was said by them of old time, Thou shalt not kill: and whosoever shall kill shall be in danger of the judgment:
22. But I say unto you, That whosoever is angry with his brother without a cause shall be in danger of the judgment: and whosoever shall say to his brother, Ra'-ca shall be in danger of the council: but whosoever shall say, Thou fool, shall be in danger of hell fire.
23. Therefore if thou bring thy gift to the altar, and there rememberest that thy brother hath ought against thee;
24. Leave there thy gift before the altar and go thy way; first be reconciled to thy brother, and then come and offer thy gift.
25. Agree with thine adversary quickly, whiles thou art in the way with him; lest at any time the adversary deliver thee to the judge, and the judge deliver thee to the officer, and thou be cast into prison.
26. Verily, I say unto thee, Thou shalt by no means come out thence, til thou hast paid the uttermost farthing.

Teach By Example

We can't expect others to do what we will not do ourselves. If you want an employee to clean a toilet you have to be willing to show them how by doing it yourself. Unpleasant, yes, but a leader who is willing to do the most menial of tasks will show his employees how by doing it himself. Loyalty is built this way with people.

Matthew 8:5-13
5. And when Jesus was entered into Capernaum, there came unto him a centurion beseeching him.
6. And saying, Lord, my servant lieth at home sick of the palsy, grievously tormented.
7. And Jesus saith unto him, I will come and heal him.

8. The centurion answered aned said Lord, I am not worthy that thou shouldest come under my roof: but speak the word only and my servant shall be healed.

9. For I am a man under authority, having soldiers under me: and I say to this man, Go, and he goeth; and to aother, Come, and he cometh: and to my servant, Do this, and he doeth it.

10. When Jesus heard it, he marveled, and said to thos that followed, Verily I say unto you, I have not found so great faith, no not in Israel.

11. And I say unto you, That many shall come from the east and west, and shall sit down with Abraham, Isaac, and Jacob in the kingdom of heaven.

12. But the children of the kingdom shall be cast out into outer darkness: there shall be weeping and gnashing of teeth.

13. And Jesus said unto the centurion, Go thy way: and as thou hast believed, so be it done unto thee. And his servant was healed in the selfsame hour.

Know how to promote others

Humbleness

A true leader is not self-promoting but promotes his staff. He/She does not take credit for things accomplished by his/her staff. He seeks to serve others thereby teaching true greatness.

John 13:4-5
He riseth from supper , and laid aside his garments; and took a towel , and girded himself.
After that he poureth water into a basin, and began to wash the disciples feet

Humility

Matthew 11:29 (KJV)
Take my yoke upon you, and learn of me; for I am meek and lowly in heart: and ye shall find rest unto your souls.

Proverbs 15:33 (KJV)
The fear of the LORD is the instruction of wisdom; and before honour is humility.

So what is humility?

Humility defined biblically is putting others before yourself.

Philippians 2:3-8 (KJV)
³ Let nothing be done through strife or vainglory; but in lowliness of mind let each esteem other better than themselves.
⁴ Look not every man on his own things, but every man also on the things of others.
⁵ Let this mind be in you, which was also in Christ Jesus:
⁶ Who, being in the form of God, thought it not robbery to be equal with God:
⁷ But made himself of no reputation, and took upon him the form of a servant, and was made in the likeness of men:
⁸ And being found in fashion as a man, he humbled himself, and became obedient unto death, even the death of the cross.

Know how to handle success

Jesus gave specific direction on how to handle success:

Luke 16:1-13
And he said also unto his disciples, There was a certain rich man, which had a steward; and the same was accused unto him that he had wasted his goods.
² And he called him, and said unto him, How is it that I hear this of thee? give an account of thy stewardship; for thou mayest be no longer steward.
³ Then the steward said within himself, What shall I do? for my lord taketh away from me the stewardship: I cannot dig; to beg I am ashamed.
⁴ I am resolved what to do, that, when I am put out of the stewardship, they may receive me into their houses.
⁵ So he called every one of his lord's debtors unto him, and said unto the first, How much owest thou unto my lord?
⁶ And he said, An hundred measures of oil. And he said unto him, Take thy bill, and sit down quickly, and write fifty.
⁷ Then said he to another, And how much owest thou? And he said, An hundred measures of wheat. And he said unto him, Take thy bill, and write fourscore.

⁸ And the lord commended the unjust steward, because he had done wisely: for the children of this world are in their generation wiser than the children of light.

⁹ And I say unto you, Make to yourselves friends of the mammon of unrighteousness; that, when ye fail, they may receive you into everlasting habitations.

¹⁰ He that is faithful in that which is least is faithful also in much: and he that is unjust in the least is unjust also in much.

¹¹ If therefore ye have not been faithful in the unrighteous mammon, who will commit to your trust the true riches?

¹² And if ye have not been faithful in that which is another man's, who shall give you that which is your own?

¹³ No servant can serve two masters: for either he will hate the one, and love the other; or else he will hold to the one, and despise the other. Ye cannot serve God and mammon.

Do we know how to handle success Biblically?

The main points above to teach us how to handle success are:
1. Don't be wasteful.
2. Be wise.
3. Realize the people of the world may be wiser in some matters than the children of God.
4. Jesus said be friends to those with money. They may provide a place for you when you fail.
5. Understand those that are faithful with little will be faithful if you trust them with a lot.
6. Understand those that are faithless with little will be faithless with a lot.
7. If we can't be trusted with money how can we be trusted with the true riches of God?
8. Or, if we can't be trusted with what belongs to someone else who will give us our own?
9. We must make sure we understand that we cannot serve two leaders. We cannot serve God and money. A choice must be made.

Hebrews 12:1 (KJV)
Wherefore seeing we also are compassed about with so great a cloud of witnesses,
let us lay aside every weight, and the sin which doth so easily beset us, and let us run
with patience the race that is set before us,

Introduction to Strategic Waiting

Ecclesiastes 3

To every thing there is a season, and a time to every purpose under the heaven:

² A time to be born, and a time to die; a time to plant, and a time to pluck up that which is planted;

³ A time to kill, and a time to heal; a time to break down, and a time to build up;

⁴ A time to weep, and a time to laugh; a time to mourn, and a time to dance;

⁵ A time to cast away stones, and a time to gather stones together; a time to embrace, and a time to refrain from embracing;

⁶ A time to get, and a time to lose; a time to keep, and a time to cast away;

⁷ A time to rend, and a time to sew; a time to keep silence, and a time to speak;

⁸ A time to love, and a time to hate; a time of war, and a time of peace.

⁹ What profit hath he that worketh in that wherein he laboureth?

¹⁰ I have seen the travail, which God hath given to the sons of men to be exercised in it.

¹¹ He hath made every thing beautiful in his time: also he hath set the world in their heart, so that no man can find out the work that God maketh from the beginning to the end.

¹² I know that there is no good in them, but for a man to rejoice, and to do good in his life.

¹³ And also that every man should eat and drink, and enjoy the good of all his labour, it is the gift of God.

¹⁴ I know that, whatsoever God doeth, it shall be for ever: nothing can be put to it, nor any thing taken from it: and God doeth it, that men should fear before him.

¹⁵ That which hath been is now; and that which is to be hath already been; and God requireth that which is past.

16 And moreover I saw under the sun the place of judgment, that wickedness was there; and the place of righteousness, that iniquity was there.

17 I said in mine heart, God shall judge the righteous and the wicked: for there is a time there for every purpose and for every work.

18 I said in mine heart concerning the estate of the sons of men, that God might manifest them, and that they might see that they themselves are beasts.

19 For that which befalleth the sons of men befalleth beasts; even one thing befalleth them: as the one dieth, so dieth the other; yea, they have all one breath; so that a man hath no preeminence above a beast: for all is vanity.

20 All go unto one place; all are of the dust, and all turn to dust again.

21 Who knoweth the spirit of man that goeth upward, and the spirit of the beast that goeth downward to the earth?

22 Wherefore I perceive that there is nothing better, than that a man should rejoice in his own works; for that is his portion: for who shall bring him to see what shall be after him?

Strategic Waiting

Understand Results take time

John 2:1-11

And the third day there was a marriage in Cana of Galilee; and the mother of Jesus was there:
[2] And both Jesus was called, and his disciples, to the marriage.
[3] And when they wanted wine, the mother of Jesus saith unto him, They have no wine.
[4] Jesus saith unto her, Woman, what have I to do with thee? mine hour is not yet come.
[5] His mother saith unto the servants, Whatsoever he saith unto you, do it.
[6] And there were set there six waterpots of stone, after the manner of the purifying of the Jews, containing two or three firkins apiece.
[7] Jesus saith unto them, Fill the waterpots with water. And they filled them up to the brim.
[8] And he saith unto them, Draw out now, and bear unto the governor of the feast. And they bare it.
[9] When the ruler of the feast had tasted the water that was made wine, and knew not whence it was: (but the servants which drew the water knew;) the governor of the feast called the bridegroom,
[10] And saith unto him, Every man at the beginning doth set forth good wine; and when men have well drunk, then that which is worse: but thou hast kept the good wine until now.
[11] This beginning of miracles did Jesus in Cana of Galilee, and manifested forth his glory; and his disciples believed on him.

Know how to plant an idea

Understanding the parables Jesus taught is vital to any leader.

Within these parables we will find the secrets to success. Every successful leader has failed. Failure breeds success. When planting ideas all leaders realize there are some ideas that will be planted that will never achieve the desired results.

Matthew 13:3-11
3 And he spake many things unto them in parables, saying, Behold, a sower went forth to sow;
4 And when he sowed, some seeds fell by the way side, and the fowls came and devoured them up:
5 Some fell upon stony places, where they had not much earth: and forthwith they sprung up, because they had no deepness of earth:
6 And when the sun was up, they were scorched; and because they had no root, they withered away.
7 And some fell among thorns; and the thorns sprung up, and choked them:
8 But other fell into good ground, and brought forth fruit, some an hundredfold, some sixtyfold, some thirtyfold.
9 Who hath ears to hear, let him hear.

Watch the idea grow

Leaders will understand that once an idea is planted it has to be given time to grow. Success is very rarely immediate. Leaders will have patience.

Matthew 13:18-23
18 Hear ye therefore the parable of the sower.
19 When any one heareth the word of the kingdom, and understandeth it not, then cometh the wicked one, and catcheth away that which was sown in his heart. This is he which received seed by the way side.
20 But he that received the seed into stony places, the same is he that heareth the word, and anon with joy receiveth it;
21 Yet hath he not root in himself, but dureth for a while: for when tribulation or persecution ariseth because of the word, by and by he is offended.

²² He also that received seed among the thorns is he that heareth the word; and the care of this world, and the deceitfulness of riches, choke the word, and he becometh unfruitful.

²³ But he that received seed into the good ground is he that heareth the word, and understandeth it; which also beareth fruit, and bringeth forth, some an hundredfold, some sixty, some thirty.

Harvest your ideas

Finally, when it's time to harvest the idea that was planted and nurtured a leader will know the right time to harvest. Harvesting is important. Knowing when to harvest is most important. As a leader, you are responsible for watching your idea as it grows. You have to make sure it does not grow wildly and you must check that it has the ability to be utilized for its intended purpose.

Matthew 13:24-43

²⁴ Another parable put he forth unto them, saying, The kingdom of heaven is likened unto a man which sowed good seed in his field:

²⁵ But while men slept, his enemy came and sowed tares among the wheat, and went his way.

²⁶ But when the blade was sprung up, and brought forth fruit, then appeared the tares also.

²⁷ So the servants of the householder came and said unto him, Sir, didst not thou sow good seed in thy field? from whence then hath it tares?

²⁸ He said unto them, An enemy hath done this. The servants said unto him, Wilt thou then that we go and gather them up?

²⁹ But he said, Nay; lest while ye gather up the tares, ye root up also the wheat with them.

³⁰ Let both grow together until the harvest: and in the time of harvest I will say to the reapers, Gather ye together first the tares, and bind them in bundles to burn them: but gather the wheat into my barn.

³¹ Another parable put he forth unto them, saying, The kingdom of heaven is like to a grain of mustard seed, which a man took, and sowed in his field:

³² Which indeed is the least of all seeds: but when it is grown, it is the greatest among herbs, and becometh a tree, so that the birds of the air come and lodge in the branches thereof.

³³ Another parable spake he unto them; The kingdom of heaven is like unto leaven, which a woman took, and hid in three measures of meal, till the whole was leavened.

³⁴ All these things spake Jesus unto the multitude in parables; and without a parable spake he not unto them:

35 That it might be fulfilled which was spoken by the prophet, saying, I will open my mouth in parables; I will utter things which have been kept secret from the foundation of the world.

36 Then Jesus sent the multitude away, and went into the house: and his disciples came unto him, saying, Declare unto us the parable of the tares of the field.

37 He answered and said unto them, He that soweth the good seed is the Son of man;

38 The field is the world; the good seed are the children of the kingdom; but the tares are the children of the wicked one;

39 The enemy that sowed them is the devil; the harvest is the end of the world; and the reapers are the angels.

40 As therefore the tares are gathered and burned in the fire; so shall it be in the end of this world.

41 The Son of man shall send forth his angels, and they shall gather out of his kingdom all things that offend, and them which do iniquity;

42 And shall cast them into a furnace of fire: there shall be wailing and gnashing of teeth.

43 Then shall the righteous shine forth as the sun in the kingdom of their Father. Who hath ears to hear, let him hear.

Strategic Teams

Jesus had a strategic team. Each disciple was handpicked by Jesus because of the qualities they exhibited in their lives.

What qualities do you bring to a team?

What qualities do the team mates you handpicked bring to the team?

Think strategically. Look at each individual and the qualities of their character you pick to help you lead. Your team will emulate the qualities they bring to the table. The disciples took on the characteristics of Jesus because they spent three years learning of him. Yet, individual characteristics from them are prevalent throughout the gospels.

Leaders must think strategically. In this section we will cover the significant qualities for a successful team.

Ability to Forgive

Matthew 5:38-40; 43-45; 6:12
38 Ye have heard that it hath been said, An eye for an eye, and a tooth for a tooth:
39 But I say unto you, That ye resist not evil: but whosoever shall smite thee on thy right cheek, turn to him the other also.
40 And if any man will sue thee at the law, and take away thy coat, let him have thy cloak also.

Matthew 5:43-45 (KJV)

[43] Ye have heard that it hath been said, Thou shalt love thy neighbour, and hate thine enemy.

[44] But I say unto you, Love your enemies, bless them that curse you, do good to them that hate you, and pray for them which despitefully use you, and persecute you;

[45] That ye may be the children of your Father which is in heaven: for he maketh his sun to rise on the evil and on the good, and sendeth rain on the just and on the unjust.

Matthew 6:12King James Version (KJV)

[12] And forgive us our debts, as we forgive our debtors.

Know Failure Breeds Success

The Apostle Peter is a great example of great failures and great successes with Jesus.

Matthew 16:22-24King James Version (KJV)

[22] Then Peter took him, and began to rebuke him, saying, Be it far from thee, Lord: this shall not be unto thee.

[23] But he turned, and said unto Peter, Get thee behind me, Satan: thou art an offence unto me: for thou savourest not the things that be of God, but those that be of men.

[24] Then said Jesus unto his disciples, If any man will come after me, let him deny himself, and take up his cross, and follow me.

Mark 8:32-34King James Version (KJV)

[32] And he spake that saying openly. And Peter took him, and began to rebuke him.

[33] But when he had turned about and looked on his disciples, he rebuked Peter, saying, Get thee behind me, Satan: for thou savourest not the things that be of God, but the things that be of men.

[34] And when he had called the people unto him with his disciples also, he said unto them, Whosoever will come after me, let him deny himself, and take up his cross, and follow me.

Peter had great ideas. Some ideas are great in theory but in practice it becomes difficult as Peter found.

Matthew 26:32-35King James Version (KJV)

³² But after I am risen again, I will go before you into Galilee.

³³ Peter answered and said unto him, Though all men shall be offended because of thee, yet will I never be offended.

³⁴ Jesus said unto him, Verily I say unto thee, That this night, before the cock crow, thou shalt deny me thrice.

³⁵ Peter said unto him, Though I should die with thee, yet will I not deny thee. Likewise also said all the disciples.

Mark 14:29-31King James Version (KJV)

²⁹ But Peter said unto him, Although all shall be offended, yet will not I.

³⁰ And Jesus saith unto him, Verily I say unto thee, That this day, even in this night, before the cock crow twice, thou shalt deny me thrice.

³¹ But he spake the more vehemently, If I should die with thee, I will not deny thee in any wise. Likewise also said they all.

John 13:37-38King James Version (KJV)

³⁷ Peter said unto him, Lord, why cannot I follow thee now? I will lay down my life for thy sake.

³⁸ Jesus answered him, Wilt thou lay down thy life for my sake? Verily, verily, I say unto thee, The cock shall not crow, till thou hast denied me thrice.

Peter's great failure

Matthew 26:74-75King James Version (KJV)

⁷⁴ Then began he to curse and to swear, saying, I know not the man. And immediately the cock crew.

⁷⁵ And Peter remembered the word of Jesus, which said unto him, Before the cock crow, thou shalt deny me thrice. And he went out, and wept bitterly.

Mark 14:71-72King James Version (KJV)

⁷¹ But he began to curse and to swear, saying, I know not this man of whom ye speak.

⁷² And the second time the cock crew. And Peter called to mind the word that Jesus said unto him, Before the cock crow twice, thou shalt deny me thrice. And when he thought thereon, he wept.

Luke 22:60-62 King James Version (KJV)

⁶⁰ And Peter said, Man, I know not what thou sayest. And immediately, while he yet spake, the cock crew.

⁶¹ And the Lord turned, and looked upon Peter. And Peter remembered the word of the Lord, how he had said unto him, Before the cock crow, thou shalt deny me thrice.

⁶² And Peter went out, and wept bitterly.

John 18:25-27 King James Version (KJV)

²⁵ And Simon Peter stood and warmed himself. They said therefore unto him, Art not thou also one of his disciples? He denied it, and said, I am not.

²⁶ One of the servants of the high priest, being his kinsman whose ear Peter cut off, saith, Did not I see thee in the garden with him?

²⁷ Peter then denied again: and immediately the cock crew.

Move on from failure

Why Peter?

Why not Peter?

Peter struggled with being submitted more than most. I believe that is why he was chosen to lead the church. He would understand submission on a different level than most. He would be willing to fail. Every great leader has to be willing to be a failure first.

The first example of a failure turned into a success for the Apostle Peter is:

Matthew 14:24-32

²⁴ But the ship was now in the midst of the sea, tossed with waves: for the wind was contrary.

²⁵ And in the fourth watch of the night Jesus went unto them, walking on the sea.

²⁶ And when the disciples saw him walking on the sea, they were troubled, saying, It is a spirit; and they cried out for fear.

²⁷ But straightway Jesus spake unto them, saying, Be of good cheer; it is I; be not afraid.

²⁸ And Peter answered him and said, Lord, if it be thou, bid me come unto thee on the water.

²⁹ And he said, Come. And when Peter was come down out of the ship, he walked on the water, to go to Jesus.

³⁰ But when he saw the wind boisterous, he was afraid; and beginning to sink, he cried, saying, Lord, save me.

³¹ And immediately Jesus stretched forth his hand, and caught him, and said unto him, O thou of little faith, wherefore didst thou doubt?

³² And when they were come into the ship, the wind ceased.

Because Peter had failures that we see as huge in the Bible any failure is simply a failure. What made Peter different was that he had a repentant attitude with a love for Jesus. Because of this repentant attitude and love for Jesus he had a special relationship with Jesus.

Matthew 16:18-20King James Version (KJV)

¹⁸ And I say also unto thee, That thou art Peter, and upon this rock I will build my church; and the gates of hell shall not prevail against it.

¹⁹ And I will give unto thee the keys of the kingdom of heaven: and whatsoever thou shalt bind on earth shall be bound in heaven: and whatsoever thou shalt loose on earth shall be loosed in heaven.

Peter's relationship with Jesus gave him the keys to the kingdom and the understanding of mysteries in the Bible. He understood what Jesus said in Matthew 28:19

Matthew 28:19-20 (KJV)

¹⁹ Go ye therefore, and teach all nations, baptizing them in the name of the Father, and of the Son, and of the Holy Ghost:

²⁰ Teaching them to observe all things whatsoever I have commanded you: and, lo, I am with you always, even unto the end of the world. Amen.

I believe Peter knew he would be the one to motivate people to do more for God by obeying Matthew 28:19-20 leading them into all truth on the day of Pentecost where in Acts 2 it is fulfilled. Acts 2:38 is the plan of salvation. It is where Matthew 28:19 is fulfilled. When we are baptized in Jesus name we are baptized in the name of God. There is nowhere in the Bible where anyone was baptized according to Matthew 28:19. Also in Acts 19 rebaptism was essential to salvation.

Acts 19:2-4King James Version (KJV)

2 He said unto them, Have ye received the Holy Ghost since ye believed? And they said unto him, We have not so much as heard whether there be any Holy Ghost.

3 And he said unto them, Unto what then were ye baptized? And they said, Unto John's baptism.

4 Then said Paul, John verily baptized with the baptism of repentance, saying unto the people, that they should believe on him which should come after him, that is, on Christ Jesus.

Acts 2:14-39King James Version (KJV)

14 But Peter, standing up with the eleven, lifted up his voice, and said unto them, Ye men of Judaea, and all ye that dwell at Jerusalem, be this known unto you, and hearken to my words:

15 For these are not drunken, as ye suppose, seeing it is but the third hour of the day.

16 But this is that which was spoken by the prophet Joel;

17 And it shall come to pass in the last days, saith God, I will pour out of my Spirit upon all flesh: and your sons and your daughters shall prophesy, and your young men shall see visions, and your old men shall dream dreams:

18 And on my servants and on my handmaidens I will pour out in those days of my Spirit; and they shall prophesy:

19 And I will shew wonders in heaven above, and signs in the earth beneath; blood, and fire, and vapour of smoke:

20 The sun shall be turned into darkness, and the moon into blood, before the great and notable day of the Lord come:

21 And it shall come to pass, that whosoever shall call on the name of the Lord shall be saved.

22 Ye men of Israel, hear these words; Jesus of Nazareth, a man approved of God among you by miracles and wonders and signs, which God did by him in the midst of you, as ye yourselves also know:

23 Him, being delivered by the determinate counsel and foreknowledge of God, ye have taken, and by wicked hands have crucified and slain:

24 Whom God hath raised up, having loosed the pains of death: because it was not possible that he should be holden of it.

25 For David speaketh concerning him, I foresaw the Lord always before my face, for he is on my right hand, that I should not be moved:

26 Therefore did my heart rejoice, and my tongue was glad; moreover also my flesh shall rest in hope:

27 Because thou wilt not leave my soul in hell, neither wilt thou suffer thine Holy One to see corruption.

28 Thou hast made known to me the ways of life; thou shalt make me full of joy with thy countenance.

²⁹ Men and brethren, let me freely speak unto you of the patriarch David, that he is both dead and buried, and his sepulchre is with us unto this day.

³⁰ Therefore being a prophet, and knowing that God had sworn with an oath to him, that of the fruit of his loins, according to the flesh, he would raise up Christ to sit on his throne;

³¹ He seeing this before spake of the resurrection of Christ, that his soul was not left in hell, neither his flesh did see corruption.

³² This Jesus hath God raised up, whereof we all are witnesses.

³³ Therefore being by the right hand of God exalted, and having received of the Father the promise of the Holy Ghost, he hath shed forth this, which ye now see and hear.

³⁴ For David is not ascended into the heavens: but he saith himself, The Lord said unto my Lord, Sit thou on my right hand,

³⁵ Until I make thy foes thy footstool.

³⁶ Therefore let all the house of Israel know assuredly, that God hath made the same Jesus, whom ye have crucified, both Lord and Christ.

³⁷ Now when they heard this, they were pricked in their heart, and said unto Peter and to the rest of the apostles, Men and brethren, what shall we do?

³⁸ Then Peter said unto them, Repent, and be baptized every one of you in the name of Jesus Christ for the remission of sins, and ye shall receive the gift of the Holy Ghost.

³⁹ For the promise is unto you, and to your children, and to all that are afar off, even as many as the Lord our God shall call.

Discernment

Know how to spot trouble and/or troublemakers. You should also be able to spot future leaders who typically have a tendency to find trouble like Peter. When you spot these people with guidance and prayer you should be able to see their potential in God.

Matthew 26:20-24King James Version (KJV)

²⁰ Now when the even was come, he sat down with the twelve.

²¹ And as they did eat, he said, Verily I say unto you, that one of you shall betray me.

²² And they were exceeding sorrowful, and began every one of them to say unto him, Lord, is it I?

²³ And he answered and said, He that dippeth his hand with me in the dish, the same shall betray me.

²⁴ The Son of man goeth as it is written of him: but woe unto that man by whom the Son of man is betrayed! it had been good for that man if he had not been born.

Hebrews 4:10(KJV)
For he that is entered into his rest, he also hath ceased from his own works, as God did from his.

Strategic Rest and Recuperation

Rest is exhibited at the very beginning of the Bible:

Genesis 2:2-3King James Version (KJV)
[2] And on the seventh day God ended his work which he had made; and he rested on the seventh day from all his work which he had made.
[3] And God blessed the seventh day, and sanctified it: because that in it he had rested from all his work which God created and made.

Understand Rest and Play are essential for Success

Even Jesus and the disciples got tired. What do you do when you get tired? Sometimes you must press on but there are times you must rest. This is where I have the biggest struggle. I am a workaholic. Everyone, however, needs rest and times to relax. Jesus relaxed and rested.

Mark 6:30-32
[30] And the apostles gathered themselves together unto Jesus, and told him all things, both what they had done, and what they had taught.
[31] And he said unto them, Come ye yourselves apart into a desert place, and rest a while: for there were many coming and going, and they had no leisure so much as to eat.
[32] And they departed into a desert place by ship privately.

Understand the need for Strategic Rest of the Mind

When leaders become overtired they do not think correctly. When this happens they tend to be short with those that work with them. The people that work with you will either increase your success or decrease it. If we do not rest we will become short-tempered, make mistakes and then blame others for our mistakes. We have to understand the principle of a Sabbath not just for our bodies but for our minds as well.

Mark 2:27
And he said unto them, The sabbath was made for man, and not man for the sabbath:

Understand the Value of Strategic Relaxation.

All leaders labor under a burden. For a church leader it is a burden of souls. For a business leader it is a burden of sales figures, action plans completed, employees hired, etc. Everyone needs a way to get out from under the burden of leadership. Church leaders have to know how to let Jesus take the burden from them at times so they can refresh to accomplish more for God. Business leaders also have to understand how to walk away from the pressure of being responsible for a company's success or failure.

If leaders don't relax eventually it will cost us our lives. There is a health issue with staying under pressure. Heart attacks, strokes, panic attacks, stomach ailments, etc are attributed to people who are constantly under stress. This is both business leaders and church leaders. We all have to realize the world went on before us and it will go on after us.

Matthew 11:28-30
[28] Come unto me, all ye that labour and are heavy laden, and I will give you rest.
[29] Take my yoke upon you, and learn of me; for I am meek and lowly in heart: and ye shall find rest unto your souls.
[30] For my yoke is easy, and my burden is light.

Psalm 23:1-3King James Version (KJV)
The LORD is my shepherd; I shall not want.
[2] He maketh me to lie down in green pastures: he leadeth me beside the still waters.
[3] He restoreth my soul: he leadeth me in the paths of righteousness for his name's sake.

Understand the Value of Privacy.

Every great leader realizes there are some things that cannot be shared with those that work for you or with you. You must protect your family. I do feel there are times we should be transparent. When deciding what to share you must make sure what you are sharing will have an impact in making business or church decisions. Jesus taught us in parables and by example.

Matthew 6:1-6King James Version (KJV)
6 Take heed that ye do not your alms before men, to be seen of them: otherwise ye have no reward of your Father which is in heaven.
[2] Therefore when thou doest thine alms, do not sound a trumpet before thee, as the hypocrites do in the synagogues and in the streets, that they may have glory of men. Verily I say unto you, They have their reward.
[3] But when thou doest alms, let not thy left hand know what thy right hand doeth:
[4] That thine alms may be in secret: and thy Father which seeth in secret himself shall reward thee openly.
[5] And when thou prayest, thou shalt not be as the hypocrites are: for they love to pray standing in the synagogues and in the corners of the streets, that they may be seen of men. Verily I say unto you, They have their reward.
[6] But thou, when thou prayest, enter into thy closet, and when thou hast shut thy door, pray to thy Father which is in secret; and thy Father which seeth in secret shall reward thee openly.

Matthew 6:16-18King James Version (KJV)
[16] Moreover when ye fast, be not, as the hypocrites, of a sad countenance: for they disfigure their faces, that they may appear unto men to fast. Verily I say unto you, They have their reward.
[17] But thou, when thou fastest, anoint thine head, and wash thy face;
[18] That thou appear not unto men to fast, but unto thy Father which is in secret: and thy Father, which seeth in secret, shall reward thee openly.

Matthew 24:3-7King James Version (KJV)

^{3} And as he sat upon the mount of Olives, the disciples came unto him privately, saying, Tell us, when shall these things be? and what shall be the sign of thy coming, and of the end of the world?

^{4} And Jesus answered and said unto them, Take heed that no man deceive you.

^{5} For many shall come in my name, saying, I am Christ; and shall deceive many.

^{6} And ye shall hear of wars and rumours of wars: see that ye be not troubled: for all these things must come to pass, but the end is not yet.

^{7} For nation shall rise against nation, and kingdom against kingdom: and there shall be famines, and pestilences, and earthquakes, in divers places.

Strategy of World Events in Leadership

When considering world events in leadership a leader must realize what is going on in the world will impact the company or church. Once a leader understands this they will know the importance of paying attention to world events.

Church leaders also have to understand world events in relationship to the kingdom of God. A church leader must also understand these events cannot be allowed to stop the work of God. If anything world events should propel us to do more for God, not less.

Matthew 6:25-34King James Version (KJV)
[25] Therefore I say unto you, Take no thought for your life, what ye shall eat, or what ye shall drink; nor yet for your body, what ye shall put on. Is not the life more than meat, and the body than raiment?
[26] Behold the fowls of the air: for they sow not, neither do they reap, nor gather into barns; yet your heavenly Father feedeth them. Are ye not much better than they?
[27] Which of you by taking thought can add one cubit unto his stature?
[28] And why take ye thought for raiment? Consider the lilies of the field, how they grow; they toil not, neither do they spin:
[29] And yet I say unto you, That even Solomon in all his glory was not arrayed like one of these.
[30] Wherefore, if God so clothe the grass of the field, which to day is, and to morrow is cast into the oven, shall he not much more clothe you, O ye of little faith?
[31] Therefore take no thought, saying, What shall we eat? or, What shall we drink? or, Wherewithal shall we be clothed?

³² (For after all these things do the Gentiles seek:) for your heavenly Father knoweth that ye have need of all these things.
³³ But seek ye first the kingdom of God, and his righteousness; and all these things shall be added unto you.
³⁴ Take therefore no thought for the morrow: for the morrow shall take thought for the things of itself. Sufficient unto the day is the evil thereof.

It is important to remember when considering world events and a strategy in dealing with them that Jesus said the following:

Revelation 3:8
I know thy works: behold, I have set before thee an open door, and no man can shut it: for thou hast a little strength, and hast kept my word, and hast not denied my name.

He followed that up by saying in,

Revelation 3:19-21
¹⁹ As many as I love, I rebuke and chasten: be zealous therefore, and repent.
²⁰ Behold, I stand at the door, and knock: if any man hear my voice, and open the door, I will come in to him, and will sup with him, and he with me.
²¹ To him that overcometh will I grant to sit with me in my throne, even as I also overcame, and am set down with my Father in his throne.

What we as leaders must is that while Jesus has set before us an open door He will not force His way into our lives. In the passage above it states, "…if any man hear my voice, and open the door, I will come in to him, and will sup with him, and he with me". It does not say Jesus will force his way in. As leaders we need to follow the example of Jesus. We need to be gentlemen and ladies when leading others. There are times we have to push a door open because we need to take care of problems. However, when doing that we should always exhibit the qualities of an ambassador.

The last verse I almost didn't include but as I read it I thought about overcoming. As a successful leader you have to be an overcomer of any type of adversity that comes your way. However, saying that, you have to realize you must again be diplomatic when you are an overcomer over others in business or church leadership. This will make or break your reputation.

As leaders our reputation has to be one of a leader who can be firm when necessary yet diplomatic when successful over others. This is very important in our strategy of world events. All business and church leaders should have a presence with political leaders. Sometimes by being present we can change policy. If you never step out, nothing will ever be accomplished.

It's time for the people of God to step out and let our national leaders know where we stand on policy making decisions. This leads us to our next section on prayer in relationship to strategy of world events.

Romans 12:12 (KJV)
Rejoicing in hope; patient in tribulation; continuing instant in prayer;

Ephesians 6:17-19 (KJV)
[17] And take the helmet of salvation, and the sword of the Spirit, which is the word of God:
[18] Praying always with all prayer and supplication in the Spirit, and watching thereunto with all perseverance and supplication for all saints;
[19] And for me, that utterance may be given unto me, that I may open my mouth boldly, to make known the mystery of the gospel,

Strategy of Prayer in World Events

To understand the strategy of prayer in world events we must first understand how to pray as Jesus taught us:

Matthew 6:9-13King James Version (KJV)
[9] After this manner therefore pray ye: Our Father which art in heaven, Hallowed be thy name.
[10] Thy kingdom come, Thy will be done in earth, as it is in heaven.
[11] Give us this day our daily bread.
[12] And forgive us our debts, as we forgive our debtors.
[13] And lead us not into temptation, but deliver us from evil: For thine is the kingdom, and the power, and the glory, for ever. Amen.

We must follow the instructions Jesus laid out. Specifically he said,
 (1) Remember the sacredness of God and his name which is Jesus.
 (2) Remember to pray for his kingdom to come.
 (3) Remember to pray for his will to be done on earth, as it is in heaven. Not our will, but his will.
 (4) Ask him for your daily bread or food.
 (5) Ask him to forgive our debts as we forgive others… oops. This is where we get in trouble. To be forgiven we must forgive.
 (6) Ask him not to lead us into temptation. That is what it says. Sometimes God may tempt us to prove us. How will you respond to that type of temptation?
 (7) Ask him to deliver us from evil.

45

(8) Finally give him glory remembering that the kingdom is his along with the power and the glory.

(9) Remember that it all belongs to him forever!

Strategy of prayer only works when we pray. Here the disciples could not understand why they could not cast out a devil. Belief + prayer = miraculous results.

Matthew 17:20-21King James Version (KJV)
[20] And Jesus said unto them, Because of your unbelief: for verily I say unto you, If ye have faith as a grain of mustard seed, ye shall say unto this mountain, Remove hence to yonder place; and it shall remove; and nothing shall be impossible unto you.
[21] Howbeit this kind goeth not out but by prayer and fasting.

I have found that when Jesus repeats himself throughout the Bible it is imperative that we pay attention. This is important. Here, in this passage, prior to the verses I have mentioned below Jesus is talking about the fig tree and the lack of fruit on it. Our prayer life should have fruit.

Does yours?

Does mine?

Matthew 21:21-23King James Version (KJV)
[21] Jesus answered and said unto them, Verily I say unto you, If ye have faith, and doubt not, ye shall not only do this which is done to the fig tree, but also if ye shall say unto this mountain, Be thou removed, and be thou cast into the sea; it shall be done.
[22] And all things, whatsoever ye shall ask in prayer, believing, ye shall receive.

Impact of World Events

When we see world events happening we need to begin to understand the scriptures and how they affect our leadership roles. We also need to pay attention to how to lead during these times. Could we do as Jesus?

Luke 6:12

And it came to pass in those days, that he went out into a mountain to pray, and continued all night in prayer to God.

Then when the following things happen we will be prepared and we will not be the one left but we will be the one taken.

Matthew 24:39-41King James Version (KJV)

[39] And knew not until the flood came, and took them all away; so shall also the coming of the Son of man be.

[40] Then shall two be in the field; the one shall be taken, and the other left.

[41] Two women shall be grinding at the mill; the one shall be taken, and the other left.

Luke 17:35-37King James Version (KJV)

[35] Two women shall be grinding together; the one shall be taken, and the other left.

[36] Two men shall be in the field; the one shall be taken, and the other left.

[37] And they answered and said unto him, Where, Lord? And he said unto them, Wheresoever the body is, thither will the eagles be gathered together.

Romans 8:25-27 (KJV)

25 But if we hope for that we see not, then do we with patience wait for it.

26 Likewise the Spirit also helpeth our infirmities: for we know not what we should pray for as we ought: but the Spirit itself maketh intercession for us with groanings which cannot be uttered.

27 And he that searcheth the hearts knoweth what is the mind of the Spirit, because he maketh intercession for the saints according to the will of God.

Revelation 5:7-9 (KJV)

7 And he came and took the book out of the right hand of him that sat upon the throne.

8 And when he had taken the book, the four beasts and four and twenty elders fell down before the Lamb, having every one of them harps, and golden vials full of odours, which are the prayers of saints.

9 And they sung a new song, saying, Thou art worthy to take the book, and to open the seals thereof: for thou wast slain, and hast redeemed us to God by thy blood out of every kindred, and tongue, and people, and nation;

Strategic Response to World Events

It is time for us to know how to respond to world events. We have to quit just watching things happen and be a participator. If we are to do as it states below:

John 14:12-14King James Version (KJV)
[12] Verily, verily, I say unto you, He that believeth on me, the works that I do shall he do also; and greater works than these shall he do; because I go unto my Father.
[13] And whatsoever ye shall ask in my name, that will I do, that the Father may be glorified in the Son.
[14] If ye shall ask any thing in my name, I will do it.

In order to do the greater works we must follow the example set before us by Jesus.

Luke 22:39-46King James Version (KJV)
[39] And he came out, and went, as he was wont, to the mount of Olives; and his disciples also followed him.
[40] And when he was at the place, he said unto them, Pray that ye enter not into temptation.
[41] And he was withdrawn from them about a stone's cast, and kneeled down, and prayed,
[42] Saying, Father, if thou be willing, remove this cup from me: nevertheless not my will, but thine, be done.

43 And there appeared an angel unto him from heaven, strengthening him.

44 And being in an agony he prayed more earnestly: and his sweat was as it were great drops of blood falling down to the ground.

45 And when he rose up from prayer, and was come to his disciples, he found them sleeping for sorrow,

46 And said unto them, Why sleep ye? rise and pray, lest ye enter into temptation.

It says that he went to the Mount of Olives to pray. This is his example. If we want access to the power we have to pray.

We have access to the power to do greater things than he did. However, will we?

Matthew 26:36-46King James Version (KJV)

36 Then cometh Jesus with them unto a place called Gethsemane, and saith unto the disciples, Sit ye here, while I go and pray yonder.

37 And he took with him Peter and the two sons of Zebedee, and began to be sorrowful and very heavy.

38 Then saith he unto them, My soul is exceeding sorrowful, even unto death: tarry ye here, and watch with me.

39 And he went a little farther, and fell on his face, and prayed, saying, O my Father, if it be possible, let this cup pass from me: nevertheless not as I will, but as thou wilt.

40 And he cometh unto the disciples, and findeth them asleep, and saith unto Peter, What, could ye not watch with me one hour?

41 Watch and pray, that ye enter not into temptation: the spirit indeed is willing, but the flesh is weak.

42 He went away again the second time, and prayed, saying, O my Father, if this cup may not pass away from me, except I drink it, thy will be done.

43 And he came and found them asleep again: for their eyes were heavy.

44 And he left them, and went away again, and prayed the third time, saying the same words.

45 Then cometh he to his disciples, and saith unto them, Sleep on now, and take your rest: behold, the hour is at hand, and the Son of man is betrayed into the hands of sinners.

46 Rise, let us be going: behold, he is at hand that doth betray me.

Know who you are in relationship to world events

An excellent leader must understand who they are Biblically before they can understand how to be an effective leader with the rights and privileges that come with leadership. We will start with understanding who Jesus is and where we fit within his kingdom.

AMBASSADORS

2 Corinthians 5:19-20King James Version (KJV)
[19] To wit, that God was in Christ, reconciling the world unto himself, not imputing their trespasses unto them; and hath committed unto us the word of reconciliation.
[20] Now then we are ambassadors for Christ, as though God did beseech you by us: we pray you in Christ's stead, be ye reconciled to God.
[21] For he hath made him to be sin for us, who knew no sin; that we might be made the righteousness of God in him.

What is an ambassador?

Simply put an ambassador is a representative of a foreign country.

Do you have any idea why you are considered an Ambassador? Let's see what the Bible says about it?

1 Peter 2:10-12King James Version (KJV)
[10] Which in time past were not a people, but are now the people of God: which had not obtained mercy, but now have obtained mercy.
[11] Dearly beloved, I beseech you as strangers and pilgrims, abstain from fleshly lusts, which war against the soul;
[12] Having your conversation honest among the Gentiles: that, whereas they speak against you as evildoers, they may by your good works, which they shall behold, glorify God in the day of visitation.

SALT OF THE EARTH

Matthew 5:13-16King James Version (KJV)
[13] Ye are the salt of the earth: but if the salt have lost his savour, wherewith shall it be salted? it is thenceforth good for nothing, but to be cast out, and to be trodden under foot of men.
[14] Ye are the light of the world. A city that is set on an hill cannot be hid.
[15] Neither do men light a candle, and put it under a bushel, but on a candlestick; and it giveth light unto all that are in the house.
[16] Let your light so shine before men, that they may see your good works, and glorify your Father which is in heaven.

It is important to remember when acting as an Ambassador we are to be loyal to our God first, then our church and then our corporation or other responsibilities.

ROYALTY

1 Peter 2:9-10King James Version (KJV)
9 But ye are a chosen generation, a royal priesthood, an holy nation, a peculiar people; that ye should shew forth the praises of him who hath called you out of darkness into his marvellous light;
10 Which in time past were not a people, but are now the people of God: which had not obtained mercy, but now have obtained mercy.

We should walk, talk, and act like royalty. There are certain things you will never see them wear. There are certain ways you will never see them act. There are certain words you will never hear them utter. It is time for leaders, whether corporate or religious, to remember who they are and act accordingly no matter where they are or what they are doing.

Leaders are always leaders. That is who you are no matter what you are doing. You must realize that and be a leader everywhere you go. Then when world events happen and you need to step up even your family and closest friends will be supporting you because your character will speak for itself.

Books authored by
Susan D Smith

Surprised by God with Pancreatic Cancer
My Child, I've Got This
Living the Miracle
Falling Back Into the Arms of God

The Blood (A novel)

Write it Upon the Doorposts of My Heart... One God

Just Tagging Along with Jesus to Kenya, Africa... the children

Depressed? What does the Bible say about it?

Will you be continue to be satisfied with less than what God has for you?

Be A Giant Among Giants

Joyful in All Things (Coming Soon)

Visa Requirements for Heaven (Coming Soon)

<u>AVAILABLE</u>

Sister Susan D. Smith
To come to your church
Or
Civic organization
To build faith and hope
(304) 640-5717

Facebook: Susan D Wine Smith
Twitter: Susaht9

www.ingramcontent.com/pod-product-compliance
Lightning Source LLC
Chambersburg PA
CBHW080553190526
45169CB00007B/2762

* 9 7 8 1 5 2 3 7 4 6 8 8 0 *